what's inside for outside cooking...

Buying the Fish, **2**
Starting the Fire, **3**
Grilled Spiny Lobster Tails, **4**
Whitefish in Foil, **4**
Charcoal Grilled Red Snapper Steaks, **4**
Flounder with Crab Stuffing, **6**
Crab Stuffing, **7**
Fisherman's Delight, **7**
Campfire Smelt, **7**
Smoked Mullet, **8**
Savory Grilled Soft-Shell Crabs, **8**
Sesame Rainbow Trout, **8**
Boiled Lobster, **10**
Charcoal Broiled Scallops, **10**
Louisiana Shrimp Boil, **11**
Scallop Kabobs, **11**
Italian Style Salmon Steaks, **11**
Fish Fry, **14**
Chesapeake Bay Clambake, **14**
Crispy Fried Rainbow Trout **14**
Oriental Swordfish Steaks, **16**
Blue Crab Boil, **16**
Ocean Perch German Potato Pancakes, **17**
Barbecued Cod Fillets, **17**
Grilled King Crab Legs, **17**
Tuna Waldorf Salad, **18**
Barbecued Halibut Steaks, **18**
Stuffed King Crab Legs, **18**
Salmonburgers, **20**
Tuna Barbecue, **21**
Hickory Smoked Sablefish, **21**
Striped Bass Supreme, **21**
Tangy Halibut Steaks, **22**
Salmon Fruit Salad, **23**
Oyster Roast, **23**
New England Clambake, **23**
Gourmet Salmon Steaks, **24**
Yellow Perch Kabobs, **24**
Zesty Lake Trout, **24**

buying the fish...

Fresh and frozen fish may be purchased in a variety of cuts or forms.

Whole or round fish are those marketed just as they come from the water. Before cooking, they must be eviscerated and scaled; usually the head, tail, scales, and fins are also removed.

Drawn fish are marketed with only the entrails removed. Before cooking, the head, scales, and fins are usually removed.

Dressed or pan-dressed fish are eviscerated and scaled; usually with the head, tail, and fins removed. This form is ready for cooking as purchased.

Steaks are cross-section cuts from larger dressed fish. They are ready to cook as purchased.

Fillets are the sides of the fish, cut lengthwise away from the backbone. They are ready to cook as purchased.

Sticks and portions are pieces of fish cut from blocks of frozen fillets with a uniform size ranging in weight from 1 to several ounces. They are ready to use as purchased.

Canned fish include many varieties of both fish and shellfish. They are ready to use as purchased.

Ask your dealer's help. When ordering fresh or frozen fish or shellfish tell your dealer how you plan to serve it. If you wish the head, tail, and fins removed from the whole or drawn fish, or if you wish the fish cut into serving-size portions, ask your dealer to do it. He will also open oysters or clams ready for serving or shuck them ready for cooking.

How much to buy. A serving of fish is generally ⅓ to ½ pound of edible fish. Therefore, for whole fish allow about 1 pound per person. For dressed fish allow ½ pound per person or 3 pounds for six people. For steaks, fillets, or sticks, allow ⅓ pound for six people.

How to know good fish. In selecting whole, fresh fish, look for bright, clear, bulging eyes; reddish pink gills; bright colored scales adhering tightly to the skin; and elastic flesh, springing back when pressed.

starting the fire...

1 Line the bottom of the fire bowl with heavy duty aluminum foil. This gives additional fuel economy by reflecting the heat and makes cleaning easier.

2 If the bottom of the fire bowl is not perforated, a gravel base will permit the fire to "breathe" and give an even-heat distribution. Use enough gravel to make the bed level out to the edge of the bowl. Gravel or crushed stones ¼ to ⅜ inch in diameter will give best results.

3 Start the fire far enough in advance to get a good bed of coals before beginning to barbecue. One method, which takes about 45 minutes, is to stack briquets in a pyramid and soak lightly with a recommended lighting fluid. Let stand 1 minute, then light. Take necessary precautions when lighting the fire.
Never use gasoline!

4 When the briquet surface is covered with a gray ash, spread the coals evenly and the fire is ready.

5 Make the charcoal layer slightly wider than the food to be cooked on the grill.

6 Wood chips give a pleasant smoky flavor to fish. Soak the chips in water at least an hour before using, so they will produce maximum smoke and not burn too rapidly. Add a few chips at a time while cooking. If chips flame up, add more wet chips.

Remember: Never overcook your fish; they contain no tough connective tissue and cook very quickly. Fish should be cooked only until they flake easily when tested with a fork.

GRILLED SPINY LOBSTER TAILS
(Front Cover)

6 spiny lobster tails (8 ounces each), fresh or frozen
¼ cup butter or margarine, melted
2 tablespoons lemon juice
½ teaspoon salt
Melted butter or margarine

Thaw frozen lobster tails. Cut in half lengthwise. Remove swimmerettes and sharp edges. Cut 6 pieces of heavy-duty aluminum foil, 12 x 12 inches each. Place each lobster tail on foil. Combine butter, lemon juice, and salt. Baste lobster meat with sauce. Bring the foil up over the lobster and close all edges with tight double folds. Make 6 packages. Place packages on a grill, shell side down, about 5 inches from hot coals. Cook for 20 minutes. Remove lobster tails from the foil. Place lobster tails on grill, flesh side down, and cook for 2 to 3 minutes longer or until lightly browned. Serve with melted butter. Serves 6.

WHITEFISH IN FOIL
(Front Cover)

2 pounds whitefish fillets or other fish fillets, fresh or frozen
2 green peppers, sliced
2 onions, sliced
¼ cup butter or margarine, melted
2 tablespoons lemon juice
2 teaspoons salt
1 teaspoon paprika
Dash pepper

Thaw frozen fillets. Cut into serving-size portions. Cut 6 pieces of heavy-duty aluminum foil, 12 x 12 inches each. Grease lightly. Place a portion of fish, skin side down, on foil. Top with green pepper and onion. Combine remaining ingredients. Pour sauce over fish. Bring the foil up over the food and close all edges with tight double folds. Make 6 packages. Place packages on a grill about 5 inches from moderately hot coals. Cook for 45 to 60 minutes or until fish flakes easily when tested with a fork. Serves 6.

CHARCOAL GRILLED RED SNAPPER STEAKS
(Opposite Page)

2 pounds red snapper steaks or other fish steaks, fresh or frozen
½ cup melted fat or oil
¼ cup lemon juice
2 teaspoons salt
½ teaspoon Worcestershire sauce
¼ teaspoon white pepper
Dash liquid hot pepper sauce
Paprika

Thaw frozen steaks. Cut into serving-size portions and place in well-greased, hinged wire grills. Combine remaining ingredients except paprika. Baste fish with sauce and sprinkle with paprika. Cook about 4 inches from moderately hot coals for 8 minutes. Baste with sauce and sprinkle with paprika. Turn and cook for 7 to 10 minutes longer or until fish flakes easily when tested with a fork. Serves 6.

FLOUNDER WITH CRAB STUFFING

6 pan-dressed flounder (¾ pound each), fresh or frozen	⅓ cup lemon juice
Crab Stuffing	2 teaspoons salt
¾ cup butter or margarine, melted	Paprika

Thaw frozen fish. Clean, wash, and dry fish. To make a pocket for the stuffing lay the fish flat on a cutting board, light side down. With a sharp knife cut down the center of the fish along the backbone from the tail to about 1 inch from the head end. Turn the knife flat and cut the flesh along both sides of the backbone to the tail allowing the knife to run over the rib bones.

Stuff fish loosely. Combine butter, lemon juice, and salt. Cut 6 pieces of heavy-duty aluminum foil, 18 x 18 inches each. Grease lightly. Place 2 tablespoons sauce on foil. Place fish in sauce. Top each fish with 1 tablespoon sauce and sprinkle with paprika. Bring the foil up over the fish and close all edges with tight double folds. Make 6 packages. Place packages on a grill about 6 inches from moderately hot coals. Cook for 25 to 30 minutes or until fish flakes easily when tested with a fork. Serves 6.

CRAB STUFFING

1 pound crab meat,
    fresh or frozen
    or
3 cans (6½ or 7 ounces each)
    crab meat
½ cup chopped onion
⅓ cup chopped celery
⅓ cup chopped green pepper
2 cloves garlic, finely chopped
⅓ cup melted fat or oil
2 cups soft bread cubes
3 eggs, beaten
1 tablespoon chopped parsley
2 teaspoons salt
½ teaspoon pepper

Thaw frozen crab meat. Drain crab meat. Remove any remaining shell or cartilage from crab meat. Cook onion, celery, green pepper, and garlic in fat until tender. Combine bread cubes, eggs, parsley, salt, pepper, cooked vegetables and crab meat; mix thoroughly.

FISHERMAN'S DELIGHT

2 pounds pan-dressed yellow
    perch or other small
    fish, fresh or frozen
2 tablespoons lemon juice
2 teaspoons salt
¼ teaspoon pepper
1 pound sliced bacon

Thaw frozen fish. Clean, wash, and dry fish. Brush inside of fish with lemon juice and sprinkle with salt and pepper. Wrap each fish with a slice of bacon. Place fish in well-greased, hinged wire grills. Cook about 5 inches from moderately hot coals for 10 minutes. Turn and cook for 10 to 15 minutes longer or until bacon is crisp and fish flakes easily when tested with a fork. Serves 6.

CAMPFIRE SMELT

3 pounds pan-dressed smelt
    or other small fish,
    fresh or frozen
2 teaspoons salt
Dash pepper
⅓ cup chopped onion
⅓ cup chopped parsley
3 strips bacon, cut in half

Thaw frozen fish. Clean, wash, and dry fish. Cut 6 pieces of heavy-duty aluminum foil, 12 x 12 inches each. Grease lightly. Divide fish into 6 portions. Place fish on foil. Sprinkle with salt and pepper. Place onion and parsley on fish. Top with bacon. Bring the foil up over the food and close all edges with tight double folds. Make 6 packages. Place packages on a grill about 4 inches from hot coals. Cook for 10 to 15 minutes or until fish flakes easily when tested with a fork. Serves 6.

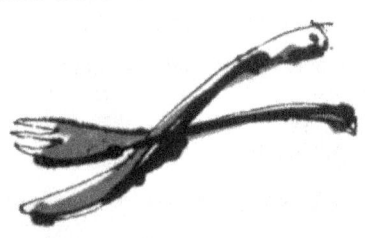

SAVORY GRILLED SOFT-SHELL CRABS

12 dressed soft-shell blue crabs, fresh or frozen
¾ cup chopped parsley
½ cup melted fat or oil
1 teaspoon lemon juice
¼ teaspoon nutmeg
¼ teaspoon soy sauce
Dash liquid hot pepper sauce
Lemon wedges

Thaw frozen crabs. Clean, wash, and dry crabs. Place crabs in well-greased, hinged wire grills. Combine remaining ingredients except lemon wedges. Heat. Baste crabs with sauce. Cook about 4 inches from moderately hot coals for 8 minutes. Baste with sauce. Turn and cook 7 to 10 minutes longer or until lightly browned. Serve with lemon wedges. Serves 6.

SESAME RAINBOW TROUT

6 pan-dressed rainbow trout or other small fish, fresh or frozen
¼ cup melted fat or oil
¼ cup sesame seeds
2 tablespoons lemon juice
½ teaspoon salt
Dash pepper

Thaw frozen fish. Clean, wash, and dry fish. Place fish in well-greased, hinged wire grills. Combine remaining ingredients. Baste fish with sauce. Cook about 4 inches from moderately hot coals for 8 minutes. Baste with sauce. Turn and cook for 7 to 10 minutes longer or until fish flakes easily when tested with a fork. Serves 6.

SMOKED MULLET
(Opposite Page)

6 dressed mullet (1 pound each) or other dressed fish, fresh or frozen
1 cup salt
1 gallon water
¼ cup salad oil

Thaw frozen fish. Remove the head just below the collarbone. Cut along the backbone almost to the tail. The fish should lie flat in one piece. Clean and wash fish. Add salt to water and stir until dissolved. Pour brine over fish and let stand for 30 minutes. Remove fish from brine and rinse in cold water.

To smoke the fish, use a charcoal fire in a barbecue grill with a cover or hood. Let charcoal fire burn down to a low, even heat. Cover with ⅓ of the wet chips.*

Place fish on a well-greased grill, skin side down, about 4 inches from the smoking coals. Cover and smoke for 1½ hours. Add remaining chips as needed to keep the fire smoking.

Increase the temperature by adding more charcoal and opening the draft. Brush fish with oil. Cover and cook 15 minutes longer. Brush fish again with oil. Cover and cook 10 minutes longer or until fish is lightly browned. Serves 6.

---

*Note: Soak 1 pound of hickory chips or sawdust in 2 quarts of water overnight.

BOILED LOBSTER

6 live lobsters (1 pound each)
1½ gallons water
⅓ cup salt
Melted butter or margarine

Pour water into a large kettle. Add salt. Cover and bring to the boiling point over hot coals. Plunge lobsters headfirst into the boiling water. Cover and simmer for 20 to 25 minutes, depending on size of lobster. Drain. Crack claws. Serve with melted butter. Serves 6.

CHARCOAL BROILED SCALLOPS

2 pounds scallops, fresh or frozen
½ cup melted fat or oil
¼ cup lemon juice
2 teaspoons salt
¼ teaspoon white pepper
½ pound sliced bacon
Paprika

Thaw frozen scallops. Rinse with cold water to remove any shell particles. Place scallops in a bowl. Combine fat, lemon juice, salt, and pepper. Pour sauce over scallops and let stand for 30 minutes, stirring occasionally. Cut each slice of bacon in half lengthwise and then crosswise. Remove scallops, reserving sauce for basting. Wrap each scallop with a piece of bacon and fasten with a toothpick. Place scallops in well-greased, hinged wire grills. Sprinkle with paprika. Cook about 4 inches from moderately hot coals for 5 minutes. Baste with sauce and sprinkle with paprika. Turn and cook for 5 to 7 minutes longer or until bacon is crisp. Serves 6.

LOUISIANA SHRIMP BOIL
(Center Photo)

5 pounds shrimp,
    fresh or frozen
1 gallon water
1 lemon, sliced
1 small onion, sliced

½ cup salt
½ cup seafood seasoning
1 clove garlic, sliced
Seafood cocktail sauce

Thaw frozen shrimp. Pour water into a large kettle. Add seasonings. Cover and bring to the boiling point over hot coals. Add shrimp. Cover and simmer for 5 minutes. Drain. Serve with seafood cocktail sauce. Serves 6.

SCALLOP KABOBS
(Center Photo)

1 pound scallops,
    fresh or frozen
1 can (13½ ounces) pineapple
    chunks, drained
1 can (4 ounces) button
    mushrooms, drained
1 green pepper, cut into
    1-inch squares

¼ cup melted fat or oil
¼ cup lemon juice
¼ cup chopped parsley
¼ cup soy sauce
½ teaspoon salt
Dash pepper
12 slices bacon

Thaw frozen scallops. Rinse with cold water to remove any shell particles. Place pineapple, mushrooms, green pepper, and scallops in a bowl. Combine fat, lemon juice, parsley, soy sauce, salt, and pepper. Pour sauce over scallop mixture and let stand for 30 minutes, stirring occasionally. Fry bacon until cooked but not crisp. Cut each slice in half. Using long skewers, alternate scallops, pineapple, mushrooms, green pepper, and bacon until skewers are filled. Cook about 4 inches from moderately hot coals for 5 minutes. Baste with sauce. Turn and cook for 5 to 7 minutes longer or until bacon is crisp. Serves 6.

ITALIAN STYLE SALMON STEAKS
(Center Photo)

2 pounds salmon steaks or
    other fish steaks,
    fresh or frozen
2 cups Italian dressing

2 tablespoons lemon juice
2 teaspoons salt
¼ teaspoon pepper
Paprika

Thaw frozen steaks. Cut into serving-size portions and place in a single layer in a shallow baking dish. Combine remaining ingredients except paprika. Pour sauce over fish and let stand for 30 minutes, turning once. Remove fish, reserving sauce for basting. Place fish in well-greased, hinged wire grills. Sprinkle with paprika. Cook about 4 inches from moderately hot coals for 8 minutes. Baste with sauce and sprinkle with paprika. Turn and cook for 7 to 10 minutes longer or until fish flakes easily when tested with a fork. Serves 6.

FISH FRY
(Center Photo)

>2 pounds ocean perch fillets
>or other fish fillets,
>fresh or frozen
>¼ cup evaporated milk
>1½ teaspoons salt
>Dash pepper
>½ cup flour
>¼ cup yellow cornmeal
>1 teaspoon paprika

Thaw frozen fillets. Cut into serving-size portions. Combine milk, salt, and pepper. Combine flour, cornmeal, and paprika. Dip fish in milk mixture and roll in flour mixture. Fry in hot fat in a heavy fry pan about 4 inches from hot coals for 4 minutes. Turn carefully and fry for 4 to 6 minutes longer or until fish is brown and flakes easily when tested with a fork. Drain on absorbent paper. Serves 6.

CHESAPEAKE BAY CLAMBAKE
(Center Photo)

>6 dozen soft-shell clams
>12 small onions
>6 medium baking potatoes
>6 ears of corn in the husks
>12 live, hard-shell blue crabs
>Lemon wedges
>Melted butter or margarine

Wash clam shells thoroughly. Peel onions and wash potatoes. Parboil onions and potatoes for 15 minutes; drain. Remove corn silk from corn and replace husks. Cut 12 pieces of cheesecloth and 12 pieces of heavy-duty aluminum foil, 18 x 36 inches each. Place 2 pieces of cheesecloth on top of 2 pieces of foil. Place 2 onions, a potato, ear of corn, 1 dozen clams, and 2 crabs on cheesecloth. Tie opposite corners of the cheesecloth together. Pour 1 cup of water over the package. Bring foil up over the food and close all edges with tight double folds. Make 6 packages. Place packages on a grill about 4 inches from hot coals. Cover with hood or aluminum foil. Cook for 45 to 60 minutes or until onions and potatoes are cooked. Serve with lemon wedges and butter. Serves 6.

CRISPY FRIED RAINBOW TROUT
(Opposite Page)

>6 pan-dressed rainbow trout
>or other small fish,
>fresh or frozen
>¼ cup evaporated milk
>1½ teaspoons salt
>Dash pepper
>½ cup flour
>¼ cup yellow cornmeal
>1 teaspoon paprika
>12 slices bacon

Thaw frozen fish. Clean, wash, and dry fish. Combine milk, salt, and pepper. Combine flour, cornmeal, and paprika. Dip fish in milk mixture and roll in flour mixture. Fry bacon in a heavy fry pan about 4 inches from hot coals until crisp. Remove bacon, reserving fat for frying. Drain bacon on absorbent paper. Fry fish in hot fat for 4 minutes. Turn carefully and fry for 4 to 6 minutes longer or until fish is brown and flakes easily when tested with a fork. Drain on absorbent paper. Serve with bacon. Serves 6.

ORIENTAL SWORDFISH STEAKS

2 pounds swordfish steaks or other fish steaks, fresh or frozen
¼ cup orange juice
¼ cup soy sauce
2 tablespoons catsup
2 tablespoons melted fat or oil
2 tablespoons chopped parsley
1 tablespoon lemon juice
1 clove garlic, finely chopped
½ teaspoon oregano
½ teaspoon pepper

Thaw frozen steaks. Cut into serving-size portions and place in a single layer in a shallow baking dish. Combine remaining ingredients. Pour sauce over fish and let stand for 30 minutes, turning once. Remove fish, reserving sauce for basting. Place fish in well-greased, hinged wire grills. Cook about 4 inches from moderately hot coals for 8 minutes. Baste with sauce. Turn and cook for 7 to 10 minutes longer or until fish flakes easily when tested with a fork. Serves 6.

BLUE CRAB BOIL

24 live, hard-shell blue crabs
1½ gallons water
1 lemon, sliced
1 medium onion, sliced
½ cup seafood seasoning
⅓ cup salt
Melted butter or margarine

Pour water into a large kettle. Add seasonings. Cover and bring to the boiling point over hot coals. Plunge crabs into the boiling water. Cover and simmer for 15 minutes. Drain. Serve with melted butter. Serves 6.

OCEAN PERCH GERMAN POTATO PANCAKES

(Photo Page 15)

1 pound ocean perch fillets or
   other fish fillets, fresh
   or frozen
3 eggs, beaten
2 tablespoons flour
2 tablespoons grated onion
1 tablespoon chopped parsley
2 teaspoons salt
Dash nutmeg
Dash pepper
2 cups finely grated
   raw potatoes
Applesauce

Thaw frozen fillets. Skin fillets and chop finely. Combine all ingredients except applesauce; mix thoroughly. Place a well-greased griddle or fry pan about 4 inches from hot coals and heat until fat is hot but not smoking. Drop ⅓ cup fish mixture on griddle and flatten slightly with spatula. Fry 3 to 4 minutes or until brown. Turn carefully and fry 3 to 4 minutes longer or until brown. Drain on absorbent paper. Keep warm. Serve with applesauce. Serves 6.

BARBECUED COD FILLETS

2 pounds cod fillets or other
   fish fillets, fresh or
   frozen
2 tablespoons chopped onion
1 clove garlic, finely chopped
2 tablespoons melted fat or oil
1 can (8 ounces) tomato sauce
2 tablespoons sherry
½ teaspoon salt
¼ teaspoon oregano
3 drops liquid hot pepper
   sauce
Dash pepper

Thaw frozen fillets. Cook onion and garlic in fat until tender. Add remaining ingredients and simmer for 5 minutes, stirring occasionally. Cool. Cut fillets into serving-size portions and place in a single layer in a shallow baking dish. Pour sauce over fish and let stand for 30 minutes, turning once. Remove fish, reserving sauce for basting. Place fish in well-greased, hinged wire grills. Cook about 4 inches from moderately hot coals for 8 minutes. Baste with sauce. Turn and cook for 7 to 10 minutes longer or until fish flakes easily when tested with a fork. Serves 6.

GRILLED KING CRAB LEGS

3 packages (12 ounces each)
   precooked, frozen
   king crab legs
½ cup butter or margarine,
   melted
2 tablespoons lemon or
   lime juice
½ teaspoon paprika
Melted butter or margarine

Thaw frozen crab legs. Combine butter, lemon juice, and paprika. Baste crab meat with sauce. Place crab legs on a grill, flesh side down, about 4 inches from moderately hot coals. Heat for 5 minutes. Turn and baste with sauce. Heat 5 to 7 minutes longer. Serve with melted butter. Serves 6.

TUNA WALDORF SALAD
(Opposite Page)

2 cans (6½ or 7 ounces each) tuna
1 cup diced apples
½ cup chopped celery
¼ cup chopped nutmeats
½ cup mayonnaise or salad dressing
Lettuce

Drain tuna. Break into large pieces. Combine all ingredients except lettuce. Serve on lettuce. Serves 6.

BARBECUED HALIBUT STEAKS
(Opposite Page)

2 pounds halibut steaks or other fish steaks, fresh or frozen
¼ cup chopped onion
2 tablespoons chopped green pepper
1 clove garlic, finely chopped
2 tablespoons melted fat or oil
1 can (8 ounces) tomato sauce
2 tablespoons lemon juice
1 tablespoon Worcestershire sauce
1 tablespoon sugar
2 teaspoons salt
¼ teaspoon pepper

Thaw frozen steaks. Cook onion, green pepper, and garlic in fat until tender. Add remaining ingredients and simmer for 5 minutes, stirring occasionally. Cool. Cut steaks into serving-size portions and place in a single layer in a shallow baking dish. Pour sauce over fish and let stand for 30 minutes, turning once. Remove fish, reserving sauce for basting. Place fish in well-greased, hinged wire grills. Cook about 4 inches from moderately hot coals for 8 minutes. Baste with sauce. Turn and cook for 7 to 10 minutes longer or until fish flakes easily when tested with a fork. Serves 6.

STUFFED KING CRAB LEGS
(Opposite Page)

3 packages (12 ounces each) precooked, frozen king crab legs
1 can (4 ounces) mushroom stems and pieces, drained
2 tablespoons melted fat or oil
2 tablespoons flour
½ teaspoon salt
1 cup milk
½ cup grated cheese
Paprika

Thaw frozen crab legs. Remove meat from shells. Remove any cartilage and cut meat into ½-inch pieces. Cook mushrooms in fat for 5 minutes. Blend in flour and salt. Add milk gradually and cook until thick, stirring constantly. Add cheese and crab meat; heat. Fill shells with crab mixture. Sprinkle with paprika. Place stuffed crab legs on a grill, shell side down, about 4 inches from moderately hot coals. Heat for 10 to 12 minutes. Serves 6.

SALMONBURGERS

1 can (1 pound) salmon
½ cup chopped onion
¼ cup melted fat or oil
⅓ cup salmon liquid
⅓ cup dry bread crumbs
2 eggs, beaten
¼ cup chopped parsley
1 teaspoon powdered mustard
½ teaspoon salt
½ cup dry bread crumbs
⅓ cup mayonnaise or salad dressing
1 tablespoon chopped sweet pickle
6 buttered hamburger rolls

Drain salmon, reserving liquid. Flake salmon. Cook onion in fat until tender. Add salmon liquid, crumbs, egg, parsley, mustard, salt, and salmon; mix well. Shape into 6 burgers. Roll in crumbs. Fry in hot fat in a heavy fry pan about 4 inches from hot coals for 3 minutes. Turn carefully and fry for 3 to 4 minutes longer or until brown. Drain on absorbent paper. Combine mayonnaise and pickle. Place burgers on bottom half of each roll. Top with approximately 1 tablespoon mayonnaise mixture and top half of roll. Serves 6.

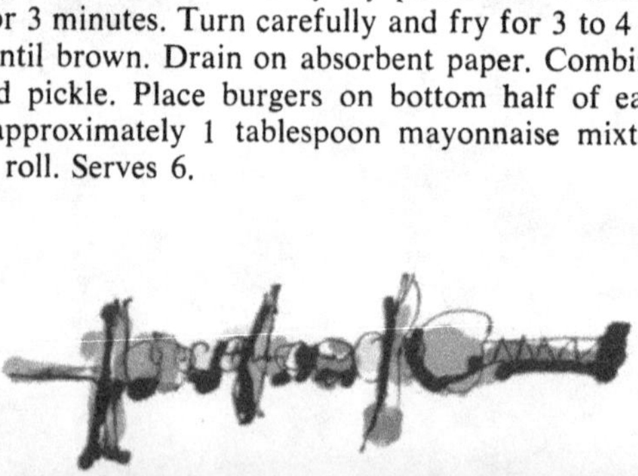

TUNA BARBECUE

(Opposite Page)

2 cans (6½ or 7 ounces
    each) tuna
½ cup chopped onion
2 tablespoons tuna oil
½ cup chopped celery
½ cup chopped green pepper
1 cup catsup
1 cup water

2 tablespoons brown sugar
2 tablespoons vinegar
2 tablespoons Worcestershire
    sauce
1 teaspoon prepared mustard
½ teaspoon salt
Dash pepper
6 hamburger rolls

Drain tuna, reserving oil. Break tuna into large pieces. Cook onion in oil until tender in a large kettle over hot coals. Add remaining ingredients except tuna and rolls. Simmer uncovered for 20 minutes, stirring frequently. Add tuna and simmer 10 minutes longer, stirring frequently. Split rolls and toast. Place approximately ½ cup tuna mixture on bottom half of roll. Cover with top half of roll. Serves 6.

HICKORY SMOKED SABLEFISH

2 pounds sablefish steaks or
    other fish steaks,
    fresh or frozen
⅓ cup soy sauce

2 tablespoons melted fat or oil
1 tablespoon liquid smoke
1 clove garlic, finely chopped
½ teaspoon ginger

Thaw frozen steaks. Cut into serving-size portions and place in a single layer in a shallow baking dish. Combine remaining ingredients. Pour sauce over fish and let stand for 30 minutes, turning once. Remove fish, reserving sauce for basting. Place fish in well-greased, hinged wire grills. Cook about 4 inches from moderately hot coals for 8 minutes. Baste with sauce. Turn and cook for 7 to 10 minutes longer or until fish flakes easily when tested with a fork. Serves 6.

STRIPED BASS SUPREME

2 pounds striped bass steaks
    or other fish steaks,
    fresh or frozen
½ cup melted fat or oil
½ cup sesame seeds

⅓ cup cognac
⅓ cup lemon juice
3 tablespoons soy sauce
1 teaspoon salt
1 large clove garlic, crushed

Thaw frozen steaks. Cut into serving-size portions and place in a single layer in a shallow baking dish. Combine remaining ingredients. Pour sauce over fish and let stand for 30 minutes, turning once. Remove fish, reserving sauce for basting. Place fish in well-greased, hinged wire grills. Cook about 4 inches from moderately hot coals for 8 minutes. Baste with sauce. Turn and cook for 7 to 10 minutes longer or until fish flakes easily when tested with a fork. Serves 6.

TANGY HALIBUT STEAKS

2 pounds halibut steaks or other fish steaks, fresh or frozen
½ cup catsup
¼ cup melted fat or oil
3 tablespoons lemon juice
2 tablespoons liquid smoke
2 tablespoons vinegar
1 teaspoon salt
1 teaspoon Worcestershire sauce
½ teaspoon powdered mustard
½ teaspoon grated onion
¼ teaspoon paprika
1 clove garlic, finely chopped
3 drops liquid hot pepper sauce

Thaw frozen steaks. Cut into serving-size portions and place in a single layer in a shallow baking dish. Combine remaining ingredients. Pour sauce over fish and let stand for 30 minutes, turning once. Remove fish, reserving sauce for basting. Place fish in well-greased, hinged wire grills. Cook about 4 inches from moderately hot coals for 8 minutes. Baste with sauce. Turn and cook for 7 to 10 minutes longer or until fish flakes easily when tested with a fork. Serves 6.

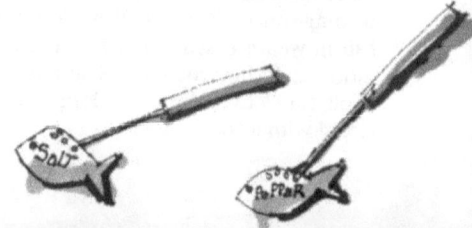

SALMON FRUIT SALAD
(Opposite Page)

1 can (1 pound) salmon
1 avocado, peeled and sliced
1 tablespoon lemon juice
2 cups orange sections
1½ cups sliced celery
½ cup toasted blanched slivered almonds
⅓ cup mayonnaise or salad dressing
Salad greens

Drain salmon. Break into large pieces. Sprinkle avocado with lemon juice to prevent discoloration. Reserve 6 avocado slices and 6 orange sections for garnish. Cut remaining avocado and orange in 1-inch pieces. Combine all ingredients except salad greens; chill. Shape into a mound on salad greens and garnish with alternate slices of avocado and orange. Serves 6.

OYSTER ROAST

36 shell oysters   Melted butter or margarine

Wash oyster shells thoroughly. Place oysters on a grill about 4 inches from hot coals. Roast for 10 to 15 minutes or until shells begin to open. Serve in shells with melted butter. Serves 6.

NEW ENGLAND CLAMBAKE
(Back Cover)

6 dozen steamer clams
12 small onions
6 medium baking potatoes
6 ears of corn in the husks
6 live lobsters (1 pound each)
Rockweed (optional)
Lemon wedges
Melted butter or margarine

Wash clam shells thoroughly. Peel onions and wash potatoes. Parboil onions and potatoes for 15 minutes; drain. Remove corn silk from corn and replace husks. Cut 12 pieces of cheesecloth and 12 pieces of heavy-duty aluminum foil, 18 x 36 inches each. Place 2 pieces of cheesecloth on top of 2 pieces of foil. Place 2 onions, a potato, ear of corn, lobster, 1 dozen clams, and rockweed on cheesecloth. Tie opposite corners of cheesecloth together. Pour 1 cup of water over the package. Bring foil up over the food and close all edges with tight double folds. Make 6 packages. Place packages on a grill about 4 inches from hot coals. Cover with hood or aluminum foil. Cook for 45 to 60 minutes or until onions and potatoes are cooked. Open packages and crack lobster claws. Serve with lemon wedges and melted butter. Serves 6.

GOURMET SALMON STEAKS
(Back Cover)

2 pounds salmon steaks or other fish steaks, fresh or frozen
1 cup dry vermouth
¾ cup melted fat or oil
⅓ cup lemon juice
2 tablespoons chopped chives
2 teaspoons salt
1 clove garlic, finely chopped
¼ teaspoon marjoram
¼ teaspoon pepper
¼ teaspoon thyme
⅛ teaspoon sage
⅛ teaspoon liquid hot pepper sauce

Thaw frozen steaks. Cut into serving-size portions and place in a single layer in a shallow baking dish. Combine remaining ingredients. Pour sauce over fish and let stand for 4 hours, turning occasionally. Remove fish, reserving sauce for basting. Place fish in well-greased, hinged wire grills. Cook about 4 inches from moderately hot coals for 8 minutes. Baste with sauce. Turn and cook for 7 to 10 minutes longer or until fish flakes easily when tested with a fork. Serves 6.

YELLOW PERCH KABOBS
(Back Cover)

2 pounds yellow perch fillets or other fish fillets, fresh or frozen
⅓ cup French dressing
3 large, firm tomatoes
1 can (1 pound) whole potatoes, drained
1½ teaspoons salt
Dash pepper
⅓ cup melted fat or oil

Thaw frozen fillets. Skin fillets and cut into strips approximately 1 inch wide by 4 inches long. Place fish in a shallow baking dish. Pour dressing over fish and let stand for 30 minutes. Wash tomatoes. Remove stem ends and cut into sixths. Remove fish, reserving dressing for basting. Roll fillets and place on skewers alternately with tomatoes and potatoes until skewers are filled. Place kabobs in well-greased, hinged wire grills. Add salt, pepper, and remaining dressing to fat; mix thoroughly. Baste kabobs with seasoned fat. Cook about 4 inches from moderately hot coals for 4 to 6 minutes. Baste with sauce. Turn and cook for 4 to 6 minutes longer or until fish flakes easily when tested with a fork. Serves 6.

ZESTY LAKE TROUT
(Back Cover)

2 pounds lake trout fillets or other fish fillets, fresh or frozen
¼ cup French dressing
1 tablespoon lemon juice
1 tablespoon grated onion
2 teaspoons salt
Dash pepper

Thaw frozen fillets. Cut into serving-size portions and place in well-greased, hinged wire grills. Combine remaining ingredients. Baste fish with sauce. Cook about 4 inches from moderately hot coals for 8 minutes. Baste with sauce. Turn and cook for 7 to 10 minutes longer or until fish flakes easily when tested with a fork. Serves 6.

☆ U.S. GOVERNMENT PRINTING OFFICE : O—817—037

www.ingramcontent.com/pod-product-compliance
Lightning Source LLC
Chambersburg PA
CBHW031440040426
42444CB00006B/908